I0494018

The Quick Guide to Telemarketing Outsourcing

ROB O'MALLEY

Copyright © 2014 Rob O'Malley

All rights reserved.

ISBN: 1496019288
ISBN-13: 978-1496019288

CONTENTS

1   Introduction   Page 1

2   Industry Analysis   Page 3

3   Project Planning   Page 9

4   Pricing   Page 13

5   Differentiators   Page 17

6   RFPs and Site Visits Page 19

7   Legal Issues   Page 25

8   Vendor Management   Page 27

9   Onshore or Offshore   Page 29

10   Conclusion   Page 31

11   Terminology   Page 33

1 INTRODUCTION

From the outside, the outsourcing of telemarketing activity to a 3rd party organisation seems like a very simple process. In reality, the opposite is true. The outsourced telemarketing industry is a high complex and diverse industry which spans multiple continents. The failure rate for outsourced telemarketing projects for British businesses is very high. However, it is not all doom and gloom. If we examine those projects which succeed, you will see a series of commonalities. If you apply these principles, you will see your success rate increase dramatically. This book looks at those principles in detail and gives practical advice on how to implement them.

If done correctly, telemarketing typically achieves far higher results when done in an outsourced environment compared with in-house operations. From the outside, it seems like a fairly simple process to outsource such activity. In reality, the opposite is true. The outsourced telemarketing industry is a highly complex and diverse industry which spans multiple continents.

The failure rate for outsourced telemarketing projects for British businesses is very high. However, it is not all doom and gloom. If we examine those projects which succeed and which fail, you will see a series of commonalities. If you apply the principles of those which succeed, you will see your success rate increase dramatically. This book looks at those principles in detail and gives practical advice on how to implement them.

I have written this book from the basis of a British company who are a potential user of outsourced telemarketing services from concept to delivery. It will guide you through the status of the industry and the types of companies involved within it. One of the key challenges for any company is to find the most suitable vendor. I have therefore included a number of chapters which map out the process from preparation to vendor selection in chronological order.

If you examine the companies which succeed in outsourcing their telemarketing, you will see detailed planning and a certainty in what they are trying to achieve. They do a series of tasks which might seem quite basic but they plan, measure and act in a highly meticulous and often ruthless way. Within this book, I will detail the areas you need to focus on. It is these areas that those who fail overlook, often believing that they are unimportant. However, it is these areas which guarantee a structure which outsourced vendors will respect, which will reduce compliance related issues and which will dramatically increase the chances of success for your outsourced telemarketing project.

This book is not intended to demonstrate how to conduct telemarketing itself. In itself, that would constitute an entire book on its own. The purpose of this book is to demonstrate how to find and manage a telemarketing company which will do this for you.

As I know everyone has limited time, I've condensed this book into a condensed form highlighting the major issues. I have backed it up with a series of templates and guides on a special website www.contactcentres.org You may also contact me in The UK on 077400 96598 or email rob.omalley@call-centres.com I am always willing to help.

2 INDUSTRY ANALYSIS

The telemarketing industry in The UK really started to take shape in The 1980s. Small, locally owned companies established themselves often using basic telephones and paper systems to manage the process. The industry grew at quite a rapid pace and the more ambitious companies invested in technology to make the process both more efficient and effective. Some of the companies started to offer other services especially inbound call handling. For many companies, inbound seemed like an easier business model to grow and so they focused more of their resources in that area. Small companies continued to establish themselves and the larger companies grew their outbound capabilities to support an increasing number of blue-chip companies who were looking at the telephone as a key channel to communicate with potential and existing companies. By the mid-1990s, foreign companies (predominantly from The United States) were buying some of the larger UK call centre companies. The volume of telemarketing calls to consumers was increasing dramatically and consumers were demanding legislation to cope with this. As a result, The Telephone Preference Service was introduced which prohibited unsolicited calls to homes which had opted out of receiving such calls. At the turn of the century, offshore call centres started to boom based on dramatic savings over their British based competitors. The UK based companies were forced to change to cope with this competition which led to tightening margins and an increase in outcome based pricing. In order to succeed, the British based call centres had to improve the quality of their offering and move away from low value work. Those companies who were unable to improve their offering found themselves out of business. The largest of these was Garlands Call Centres which had previously been a highly successful company but had failed to respond the dramatically transformed market conditions. The growth of offshore had led to over-capacity in the UK sector but the companies who survived have come out as stronger, more efficient businesses and a greatly improved service offering. The rise of low cost offshore call centres had dramatically increased the number of telemarketing calls each household was receiving and this in turn was leading to exponential growth in the number of subscribers to The

Telephone Preference Service. Households were also becoming far more resistant to telemarketing calls especially the low quality ones being delivered from Asia. Legislation and regulations also started to increase their significance in the period 2004-2011 and there here was increased implementation of the laws governing both unsolicited and silent calls. In addition, a number of industries strengthened their regulations regarding telemarketing. Ever-reducing conversion rates offshore together with negative brand sentiment around offshore call centres and the increased chance of legal and regulatory repercussions has led to much of the higher value telemarketing work being brought back to The UK. Many of India's low-tiered telemarketing companies have gone out of business because low value telemarketing no longer works.

All of this has led us to the nature of industry we have today. Gone are the days when telemarketing was simply a numbers game. The likelihood of success for onshore telemarketing is far higher than offshore but so are the costs. The demand for onshore telemarketing has increased over recent years but the market has changed. Clients are now far more sophisticated in their vendor selection and management processes and consumers offer a dramatically reduced window on each and every call. The successful onshore telemarketing companies have also improved their offering with things such as the increased use of analytics, effective performance management strategies& technologies designed specifically to aid both the agent and the overall process. There is still a demand for offshore call centres but this now requires very careful consideration.

The telemarketing industry which now exists covers a whole range of different activities which form part of the sales and/or marketing functions. These can broadly be categorized into the following:

- Information gathering: This covers a number of areas such as cold contacting customers to obtain certain information and contacting past or existing customers to confirm and/or update existing information

- Generating leads: This involves the contacting of existing or potential customers to pre-qualify them and establish a pre-specified level of interest for further contact by sales people either in the form of a telesales call or a face to face appointment.

- Making sales: This involves the closing of a sales to a customer which normally requires no or minimal post-call contact. In some circumstances, this will involve receiving a payment or a promise to pay.

-Courtesy Calls – These are calls made following on from a sale or other positive action designed to assist the customer and to provide a positive opinion of the company. In some such calls, there may be an opportunity to up-sell or cross-sell an additional product or service

Some vendors will choose to specialize in one of the above areas where most will offer services across the spectrum. For the smaller telemarketing companies, you will find that their current client base tends to focus in one of those areas. This area effectively becomes the sweet spot for that company. A telemarketing company which specializes in courtesy type calls does not necessarily lend itself well to sales calls and with so many competing telemarketing companies, it makes sense to choose a vendor with the most relevant experience.

Not only does the type of work conducted vary dramatically but so does the types of business which conduct this work. To fully understand the outsourced telemarketing industry, you need to be able to different types of company of which it is made up. There are 8 different types of companies which can be grouped as follows:

-Global – These are the outsourced vendors which operate in multiple geographies. They are predominantly owned by parent companies from The United States, Europe or India. Outbound tends to constitute a much smaller percentage of their overall business compared with customer services. Some of them will not offer telemarketing services or may only do so for specific clients. Most of them will offer outbound services delivered either from their UK operations or their offshore facilities. However, there are some who don't or who will only offer telemarketing services to clients who procure other key services from them. They tend to have superior technologies and processes compared with their smaller equivalents. They will often have minimum requirements for the size of project and will sometimes only be interested in projects for blue-chip clients. Some of them will charge a premium for their services.

-Independents - These are the larger UK owned vendors who typically only have a UK location but may have a partnership with an offshore based vendor. They will generally have good technologies and processes. Given that telemarketing projects are normally country-specific as opposed to global deals, they tend to have a greater percentage of their business focussed on outbound. However, the individual companies within this group vary dramatically from each other. They will normally have globally and nationally recognised accreditations which may be essential in some industries.

-Total Outsourcers – These are companies who cover multiple outsourcing sectors such as ITO outsourcing or back office outsourcing. These include companies like Capita. Whilst they will generally offer telemarketing services, it will often not be a core competency and will typically not have a specialisation in outbound telemarketing.

-Bureaus – These are small vendors operating from the UK who have a number of small clients. They are often 100% inbound or 100% outbound. The size of their clients is generally quite small. Technology will be weak in these vendors but they tend to offer a more personal service. They are sometimes referred to as niche players.

-Micro – These are very small companies either operating from a home location or small low-cost office base. They will generally only work on outbound based applications. They are almost always owner operated. They will normally have low end technology and no scale of operations. They will generally operate with projects of 1-2 people and sometimes may divide their agents' time between multiple clients.

-Offshore (Low Tiered) – There are literally 1000s of call centres in locations such as India, South Africa & The Philippines who offer telemarketing services. Low tiered offshore call centres will sell their services at very low rates but will generally have poor people, processes and technology.

-Offshore (Mid Tiered). These are more expensive than their low tiered equivalents but will have better technology, processes and people but still well below the domestic and global outsourcers. Their prices will be more expensive than their low tiered equivalents but normally slightly lower than the offshore operations of the global outsourcers.

-Specialist – Specialist call centres are ones which specialise in a specific type of work or industry. Many of these will be outbound telemarketing specialists in industries such as technology or financial services. Most of these are small and as such possess many of the same characteristics as the bureau/niche call centres.

3 PROJECT PLANNING

There is a direct correlation between the quality of the preparation and the success of an outsourced telemarketing project. The planning and preparation will go through many phases. The initial phase is to determine who within your organization will be involved with the planning & vendor selection process. This is essential because one of the major reasons for telemarketing projects to fail is the lack of internal support on the client side. By engaging with the concerned parties at the early stage, the project has a much higher likelihood of success. You will also become aware of any potential areas of concern at an earlier stage. For larger projects, the responsibilities may be something like this:

	Procurement	Operations	Financ e	Executiv e	Marketin g
Process Definition	X	X			
Research	X				
PQQ	X	X	X		X
Shortlist	X	X	X		X
RFP Preparation	X				
RFP Evaluations	X	X	X		X
Shortlist	X	X	X		X
Site Visit	X	X	X	X	X
Evaluation	X	X	X	X	X
Decision			X	X	

For smaller projects or projects within smaller organizations, there is likely to be fewer processes involved and less people.

The next step is to determine the specifics of the work you wish to outsource. This will help to form your initial project briefing for both internal and external use. This is called the "process definition". The process definition decides on a number of key factors including the following:

- An overview of the project

- The aims and objectives of the program

- The timescales involved

- The volumes (numbers of calls, sales, outcomes or personnel required)

-The key performance indicators required/anticipated

The process definition can be as long or short as you choose at this stage but it is advisable to keep it relatively short (less than 2 pages).

After you have written this document, it's time to start finding the most suitable call centres. To start with, you need to determine a number of characteristics of your ideal call centre(s) for this project. These are the kind of questions you should be asking:

-Should this be done onshore on offshore?

-What size of business you feel is most appropriate?

-Do you require any specific accreditations?

-What specific skills/experience/technologies do you require?

These days, the decision about whether the work should be done onshore or offshore is a fairly easy one to make. It is for this reason that detailed analysis of the onshore v offshore debate has been moved to chapter 11. A company will undoubtedly experience lower results, lower data utilization, increased management requirements and more complaints and compliance issues when outsourcing overseas. Of course, the cost is much lower offshore and this may be the only economically viable option. For now, we will assume that you know whether this work should be done onshore or offshore. It is imperative that the decision about onshore v offshore is made at this stage. Failure to do so will make the vendor selection process far more complex.

Once you have made the decision as to whether this work will be kept onshore or not, it's time to research the most suitable call centre for your needs. Of course, in a market where there are so many call centres, it's often difficult to make a shortlist simply based on the information available on the internet. You may wish to use the vendor finder service available at www.contactcentres.org where you type in some details about your project and they present you with a number of companies who fit the criteria you are looking for. There is no definite number as to the number of companies you wish to engage at this process but remember that the more companies you shortlist at this stage, the more work which will be involved in the vendor evaluation process. If you are unsure of your overall strategy at this stage, it would be a good idea to select different types and size of vendor. For example, if you believe that you should work with a bureau call centre, you might want to include 6 or 7 of these and 1 larger centre as a wild card in the process. This will enable you to get a different perspective on certain areas and maybe to discover some new ideas. I've seen many occasions where the client ends up choosing the "wildcard". Some companies opt to work with a consultant or a broker at this stage. There are a number of highly reputable consultants who will assist you in short listing potential vendors. They will either charge you a fee for their services or will take a pre-agreed commission from the telemarketing company as a finders fee.

4 PRICING

Before you send out your request for a proposal or a request for a quotation, it is important to have an understanding of the pricing mechanism you would like to employ. In 2013, I was conducting a consultancy process for a client who wanted to outsource a large call centre. We received a total of 20 responses to the RFP and within that; we had 12 different pricing structures. It is important that the RFP process is designed to force vendors to compare on a like for like basis and so you should have an understanding of the way you would like prices to operate.

There are many different pricing structures but for ease of explanation, the pricing structures can be split into 2 different groups; the first group is pricing structures based on units of call centre agent time. The second group is pricing structures which are based on outcomes. There are of course hybrid mechanisms of these 2 structures and many different components within each group.

Pricing Per Agents

Common pricing mechanisms include a cost per FTE per month or a cost per agent hour. However, the way in which this figure is calculated can vary dramatically. For example, some vendors charge for on a timesheet and others on a productive hour. The timesheet hour rate means that a client is charged for every hour that is on a call centre agent's timesheet. A productive hourly rate means that the client is not charged only for the hours where the agent is ready and able to take or make telephone calls.

Pricing Per Outcomes

Outcome based pricing is where the client pays the telemarketing per agreed action or outcome. In survey work, this might involve a payment per question or per completed survey. In appointment setting, it may mean a price per appointment and in sales, a fee per sale. In many cases, the price per sale will be dependent on a number of factors. In some cases, there will be a hybrid pricing model based partly on agent time and partly based on outcomes.

It's fairly standard practice for the pilot or initial stages of a campaign to be based on a cost per time pricing mechanism. If we examine those companies with a high degree of success in telemarketing, they almost all do this. Companies which want to start a project based on a pure cost per outcome basis will almost experience a project failure. The best call centres will simply refuse to work on this basis. Those call centres who do wish to operate on this basis will normally fail. This is because they are unable to invest in the correct training and there will be minimal support to conduct your campaign. You will always be able to find a call centre who can service your needs but starting on a pay per performance basis will almost always involve a lot of work on your part with minimal chance of success.

Despite clear evidence that pay per performance doesn't work in the short term, telemarketing is ultimately about achieving a cost per outcome and a return on investment. What you should look to do is a minimal trial of 12 weeks where you pay on a cost per hour basis. This will give the call centre the time to invest in the important things such as agent training and compliance. It will also add in areas such as script development and iron out the procedures.

Typical Rates

A typical rate for a telemarketing agent in The UK is typically between £140 & £160 per agent per day. There may be some lower prices for larger projects and for lower quality call centres. There may be additional costs associated where more complex skills are required. In terms of a cost per hour, this equates to about £22 on a productive hour and £19 on a sign-on-hour basis. When charging on an outcome based model, the outsourced vendor will look to make slightly more when calculating it back to a "per-hour" basis to accommodate for the additional risk associated with these pricing models.

Offshore, the rates vary dramatically. I have seen prices from as low as $5 per hour quoted for low tiered call centres but they will generally offer a very poor service. We have seen quotes from some South African call centres as high as £13 per hour. Typical rates for a good quality call centre in India or The Philippines is in the region of £8-£10 per hour.

It's important to remember that the rates I've discussed are headline rates and the ways in which vendors charge and what they charge for varies dramatically. In order to effectively evaluate, the Request for Proposal or Request for Quotation that you send out to potential vendors should work on a total cost basis. A total cost basis includes all associated costs such as:

-Account Management and reporting

-Telecommunications

-Incentives

- Quality control and team leaders.

-Software and technology

-Data transfer

You are then charged a unit cost for the time of the call centre agents with all other costs rolled into this. You can choose what that pricing unit is and clearly document it. Potential vendors are then asked to quote for their services on a like-for-like basis for ease of comparison.

Set Up Costs

The outsourced vendor will always incur some costs involved in setting up a telemarketing project. These costs include the training of agents and the setting up of technology. Where there is a small amount of time and money involved, the vendor will either absorb these costs or will charge them at a reduced rate to cover costs. For more complex projects involving extensive training, there are likely to be costs associated with this.

5 THE DIFFERENTIATORS

Before going through the formal vendor selection process, it's important to determine what makes a good telemarketing company. For those new to outsourcing such work, differentiating between call centres can seem a very difficult task. After all, a call centre can seem like a homogenous product. They are simply a group of people sat on telephones behind a computer backed up some type of management structure. However, in my many years of working with outsourced telemarketing companies, I can tell you that there are a number of commonalities between those who normally succeed and those who normally fail. In many ways, this is the most important chapter of the book as it provides a huge insight from many of my former clients which is not otherwise available.

Length of Clients:

It's important to assess the current clients of a call centre to see how long they've been with that vendor. It's actually relatively easy for a call centre to win business but it's much harder to keep them. If you look at a company where are of their clients have been with them for less than a year, then there is probably a very good reason for this.

Focus on outbound:

There are plenty of companies in The UK who offer telemarketing in addition to a whole range of other services. For many, this may mean other call centre services such as customer services or technical support work. There are others who also offer other services completely unrelated to telemarketing but offer such services as a stand-alone offering. However, telemarketing is a very specialized discipline and those companies for whom it is not a significant part of their business typically lack the focus to make a success of it. As a rule of thumb, I recommend that the company's UK revenues should be at least from 50% from telemarketing. If this isn't the case, there is a much higher likelihood of failure.

Data and Analytics

Telemarketing without an in-depth understanding of data and the analysis of data is like having a car without an engine. It's always worth remembering that if you choose a good telemarketing company, they are far more than simply a resource to provide people who provide people to make phone calls. A good call centre should be able to provide you with a whole range of advice including everything from script development to overall telemarketing strategy. However, if there is one area where some call centres really shine, it is an in-depth understanding of data and analytics. The sheer volume of telemarketing calls received by consumer and businesses has made telemarketing much more challenging. The days of calling plenty of people and hoping that enough of them will buy your product or service has long gone. A good telemarketing company will know the most likely people to be interested in your product or service, the best time to call them and which of your products or services to pitch to them.

You will find that most telemarketing companies will say that their people are their differentiators. Of course, the quality of the agents is a key component of the success of a project but the evidence suggests that there really isn't a major difference between the quality of agents from vendor to vendor within UK call centres. Offshore, there is a larger difference in agent quality between high and low tiered vendors. This is because the higher tiered vendors will generally pay higher salaries and will have far more robust recruitment and assessment processes.

6 RFPS & SITE VISITS

The next logical step is to produce a Request for Proposal to send out to the potential vendors you have chosen. In the outsourcing of customer service activity, an RFP is used in the vast majority of cases. In telemarketing, they are used far less often. However, it is proven that clients who go through such a process for telemarketing are far more likely to find a vendor who fulfils their requirements due to a number of reasons:

- It enables you to compare vendors on a like for like basis.

- It provides a formal framework and enables both the client and vendor to give the process detailed consideration

- It ensures that you are paying the right price for your services

- It can often raise additional opportunities and/or threats

The RFP document itself does not need to be extensive but it does have to include the aspects which are relative to your work. At www.contactcentres.org we have some template RFPs which you are free to use and adapt.

The RFP would normally include the following sections:

- Details of the RFP process: including any required formats, relevant dates (including confirmation of interest and final submission date), how to ask any questions, who to send the final response to & the process once the RFP has been submitted.

- A Project Brief: Detailing information about your company, your products/services, the scope of the project, anticipated results, details of similar past work.

- General Vendor & Contact Information: This would include details such as the size of the telemarketing company, company name, address and contact details for the point person during the evaluation phase.

-Experience: This section seeks to examine the experience of the vendor in relation to the work to be outsourced. This section would normally ask to explain examples of current or recent work performed. Always ask for the duration these contracts are in place. The best call centres are the ones who can keep their contracts for a long period.

- Recruitment and Training: Explanations of how the vendor would find the right people. Questions such as whether they would be internally sourced or external are normally asked. This section would also ask questions in relation to the soft skills training the call centre agents receive & how client specific training would be delivered. You also need to ascertain the quality of the training function as it relates to your work.

- Operational Management: This covers a wide range of activities such as how performance is managed, how issues are dealt with, reporting and anything else relevant to your project.

-Technology: This includes how data is stored, transmitted & managed, specifications of dialling equipment, applications used and how clients own systems are accessed or integrated.

- Quality & Compliance: How quality is measured and remedial action taken. It also includes how the vendor would cope with legal & regulatory issues. This section would normally ask for any relevant externally awarded accreditations

Where you require minimal information, it is normal to give approximately 2 weeks to complete the RFP and up to 6 weeks for very large submissions.

Prior to sending out the RFP, you should have determined how the RFPs will be assessed. Normally, each section is given a weighting. There is no definite rule as to which section requires the greater weighting. This is very much a process relevant to each company. For some companies, matching the culture of the vendor with that of the client is the most important aspect. For some, it has very minimal relevance. It's best practice to use a scoring sheet in the form of a simple Excel form to enable you to rank each call centre against each criteria. On www.contactcentres.org we have a template. Of course each company's rankings are different but the template we've used is a standard one which gives higher weightings to areas such as experience and operational management. The results of every person involved in the decision making process and the averages should be recorded and analysed. You will often find that one person has a result for one or two of the centres which is dramatically different to everyone else & there are normally a number of reasons for this. Sometimes, the individual has a specific concern about the centre or the individuals within that organisation which may or not be unfounded. It may be that this individual has a specific thought process about the type of company he/she wants to work with. Whatever the reason for their scoring, it's important to address it as not having everyone on board can make it harder to deliver with an outsourced partner.

Once you have analysed your scoring sheets, it's time to decide which companies to shortlist for a site-visit. It may be that there is 1 stand-out vendor based on your responses. In these cases, you may decide that you only want to visit 1 centre in order to verify the information you have to date. You may visit a 2nd call centre simply to benchmark against your primary choice vendor.

However, best practice suggests that you should visit 3-5 potential vendors. These visits should be held at the location where the calling activity will take place. This is crucial as some vendors have different cultures & skills within each site. The ideal time to visit the operation is during the times which would be your peak times of operation. If conducting offshore site visits in Asia, this is likely to be during the night.

Before make the site visit, you should remember the following things:

-Have clear objectives as to what is expected from the site visit
-Spend as little time as possible in a meeting room and maximise time within the call centre operation
-Meet the people who would be directly involved in your work
-Measure the centre against pre-determined criteria

As with the RFP process, the sites should be judged against pre-determined criteria. This is most likely to be exactly the same criteria as with the RFP process.

Despite the apparent similarities between the RFP & the site visit processes, the bulk of the site visit should be in areas not covered in the RFP process. It is an opportunity to get an idea of the culture which exists with the outsourced vendor and more importantly to meet the key people involved. It is also an opportunity for additional clarification of the areas covered in the RFP process.

One area where potential clients often get carried away in the site visit is the office layout. Rather than focus on the first impressions of a call centre, there are some aspects you should look for as follows:

- Does the office offer a good working environment for employees?
- Is the area organised?
- How is security?
- Is there evidence of a clear performance management program?
- Is there evidence of coaching?
- How do you feel about the quality of people who will be managing your work?
- Where would your work be located within the call centre? Is there available capacity?
- Always discuss pricing to see if there is any flexibility

It's important to keep an open mind at the end of each site. Always record your findings from each visit as this will enable you to make a rational decision.

Although I always consider a site visit to be an essential part of the vendor selection process, there are some times when this may be impractical. For example, if you have very tight timescales, if the project is very small or if you are outsourcing overseas and are unable to justify the travel expenses. In all of these cases, there are some ways to work round the process. If you have very tight timescales, you should combine the RFP & Site Visits by ensuring that all key people are at the site visit and obtaining all the information you need in one go. For smaller projects are offshore work, you should always consider using a service to find you a qualified centre. If you use one of the forms on www.contactcentres.org you will find call centres that have been pre-screened for such projects.

By the time you have gone through this stage, you should have a call centre which meets your criteria and with whom you have negotiated payment terms with which all parties are comfortable. Before starting on a project, you need to have performed the relevant due diligence before moving onto the legal considerations. The due diligence would involve the following:

-Taking up references from existing clients.
-Checking relevant accreditations (if appropriate)
- Credit checking. This is important because many smaller centres often operate on risky business models and it could pose you problems if they are unable to continue operating during operations.

7 LEGAL

Before engaging in any project, you need to seek proper legal representation to ensure that your interests are protected. Despite this, it is estimated that in 70% of projects, lawyers are not used in the formation of an agreement. In many of these cases, there will not even be a written contract signed by both parties. Whilst this section is not designed to replace professional legal representation, there are a number of legal issues which require careful consideration:

The first of these issues is the Non-Disclosure Agreements. A non-disclosure agreement prohibits the parties to the agreement from sharing confidential information. It should include the following sections.

(1) Details of the contracting parties

(2) The purpose of the non disclosure agreement

(3) Definition(s) of what determines the information which is dealt with by the agreement

(4) Consequences for breach of the non-disclosure agreement

In most cases, the agreement will be a mutual agreement covering both the client and the outsourced vendor. The non-disclosure agreement should be agreed and signed at the earliest opportunity especially when outsourcing could impact on your internal staff.

Contractual Agreements

The formal agreement is similar to any contractual agreement. If you do not have an agreement of your own, you will find that most call centres have a standard agreement as a template which they will be happy to provide you. One of the most important things to remember about outsourcing telemarketing activity is that you remain responsible for the things that the telemarketing company does on your behalf. This means that it's essential that the agreement covers the following areas:

-It must ensure that they abide by legislation governing silent calls
- It must ensure that they abide by laws governing The Telephone Preference Service.
- They must abide by all laws governing the mis-selling of products and services
- They must ensure that data is handled according to The Data Protection Act

In each of the above examples, the agreement should document an audit process, a resolution and detail compensation for breaches of the above.

8 VENDOR IMPLEMENTATION & MANAGEMENT

The implementation of any outsourced call centre project is the time during which critical errors are most likely to occur. Telemarketing companies will typically have a process which takes a project from contract sign-off to the first call and during the initial stages of the work. However, it is still important to be engaged in this process especially as there are many touch points between the outsourced vendor and your internal resources. A project plan as a minimum should include the following:

- -Recruitment of staff (or reallocation if tenured staff are to be deployed)

- - How the training will be conducted (including any soft skills)

- -Confirming the reporting requirements

- -Determining the specifics related to quality & compliance

- - Implementing any IT processes including telephony, dialer rules, databases and data transfer between client & outsourced vendor.

- -A plan to reach the agreed the Service Level Agreements combined with plans to flag underperformance and implement appropriate corrective actions

At all stages of the project planning process, there should be a review of any potential red flags which have the potential to delay the project start date or have a negative influence on performance or compliance.

There are certain areas of the implementation process where input from the client is high valued. This is especially true in the training process where it is standard practice to either conduct a Train the Trainer (T3) session with trainer(s) from the vendor or even better to conduct the initial training session with the first agent(s).

Ongoing Management

From the outset, it is best practice to establish a series of formal interaction sessions with the outsourced vendor. This helps to focus the attention of the outsourced vendor and to ensure that key target areas are kept on track. The volume and depth of these interactions will vary according to the scale of the project you are outsourcing. For example, large scale projects might even involve a client representative being based permanently at the call centre. Small projects might only require a 10 minute call once a week unless there are any issues.

These interactions will take place with the vendor's representative. When working with very small vendors, this is likely to be either with the owner/manager of the call centre or the person in charge of the operation. When working with larger call centres, this is more likely to be with someone from the client services function such as the account manager often supported by someone from operations working on your business.

A typical ongoing management program would be something like this:

Daily: Reporting emailed to vendor by client (by 10am)

Weekly: Call (Friday 11am): Project Review (Account Manager, Team Leader & Client Representative)

Fortnightly: Call Calibration Session Project Review (Account Manager, Team Leader & Client Representative)

Monthly: Site meeting at call centre: Project Review, Update Training, Team Briefing (Account Managers, Directors, Team Leader & Client Representatives)

Quarterly Business Review: Review at call centre: (all from monthly meeting + contract reviews, project strategy)

9 ONSHORE OR OFFSHORE?

Most people involved in the decision to outsource telemarketing activity now have a clearly defined views about whether to offshore such activity or keep it in The UK. However, with the maturity of the offshore market, it is now becoming more clear which types of work are best suited to offshore and which are not.

(1) Business to Business appointment setting and sale should ALWAYS be done in The UK. I've worked with lots of clients who've tried offshore and not one has succeeded in the long-term. Just don't do it!

(2) Business to business list building, data cleansing work should generally be done offshore. It's normally about getting good quality control at a good cost and that can be done offshore assuming you have the right vendor.

(3) Business to consumer sales: There are some examples of when this has worked offshore but invariably, it's better done in The UK. The conversion rates will be higher, the costs per sale are higher, the data usage is higher, and the required input from the client is lower as are the complaints. If you are planning to offshore B2C sales work, then you should choose a tier 1 vendor as choosing a s low tiered call centres tend to be weak in sales and have weak data security

(4) Anything which requires the collection of financial information such as bank account details or credit card information is best done onshore. Consumers are especially reluctant to give such information to foreign call centres.

(5) When dealing with your existing customers or other value data, you should always do this onshore or with a high tiered offshore provider.

Which Country To Use?

The internet is full of theories about which countries are the best offshore locations. Unfortunately, these are generally written by people with a vested interest in promoting a particular country. The reality is that one location is not necessarily better than others. For example,. India is home to some of the world's best offshore call centres and is also home to some of the worst.. The level of maturity of offshoring now means that the national advantages have largely been ironed out. For example, The Philippines has a huge English-speaking population and strong communication skills. If you were setting up a call centre 10 years ago in Manila, you would have had a distinct advantage over people setting up in other countries. However, the sheer volume of call centres which now exist there have removed those natural advantages. It's therefore far more important to focus on the quality of the vendor rather than the location itself.

10 CONCLUSION

If done correctly, outsourcing your telemarketing activity will normally achieve better results than a comparative in-house operation. However, there are a number of key things to do which will improve performance.

- Always choose a provider which specializes in telemarketing
- Make the vendor selection process as formal and as transparent as possible
- Have less Key Performance Indicators (2-4) and focus heavily on them
- Always have a full audit process to check for compliance. Never rely on
- Show extreme caution when outsourcing offshore. Not only will the majority of them yield poor results but you are still liable for the way in which they deal with your data.
- Always be mindful of legislation regarding telemarketing, the handling of personal data, general laws about selling and specific rules governing your industry. You are likely to still be liable for the actions of your outsourced partner.
- Don't be overly-concerned about location. The quality of vendor is what's important.
-Personal relationships with vendors are an important component but are certainly not the most important factor in vendor selection
-Be honest with vendors at all stages of the process.
- The only way an outsourced telemarketing project will work is if it's a win-win for both the client and the vendor. Those which don't are likely to be very short-lived.
- Stay away from pay per performance pricing structures during the pilot stages. They may seem a tempting proposition but are a false promise.
-Always choose a vendor with relevant experience. Telemarketing companies a very broad spectrum of disciplines and the experience from similar work will be invaluable.

11 TERMINOLOGY

Below is some of the terminology common used in telemarketing outsourcing:

Abandoned call – in outbound terminology, an abandoned call is the same as a silent call. This is where a predictive dialler does not have any available agents

Account Manager/Account Director - Part of the Client services team within the outsourced vendor. They are responsible for liaison between the clients and internal departments at the outsourced vendor

Analytics - consists of many aspects but is normally involved around using data to determine and improve results.

Average Handle Time (AHT) – is a measure of how long it takes it deal with a particular call or other interaction. It includes the time the agent takes on the call (including in-call hold time) and any post call follow up (often referred to as Wrap time)

BDD - is short for Business Development Director. The person within the outsourced vendor responsible for winning new business.

BDM - is short for Business Development manager. The person within the outsourced vendor responsible for winning new business

Blended agent – is a call centre agent who takes both inbound and outbound calls. Inbound calls are generally prioritised and during quiet periods, outbound calls are performed.

Call centre – is an environment where multiple call centre agents make or receive phone calls. Other terms include contact centre, interaction, customer service centre or telemarketing centre.

Call centre agent – is an employee who makes or receives calls to/from customers.

Call forecasting - is the process of determining the volume of calls expected to be made on a monthly or even daily basis

Captive centre – is the term used to describe a client's in-house call centre as opposed to the outsourced environment.

Call monitoring – is the process of listening to calls either locally or in a remote environment.

Champion Challenger – is where a client uses one or more call centres to compete against each other and/or a captive call centre.

Client Services - is the Department responsible for dealing with the client

Cross media queuing – is a part of unified communications which enables all interaction types (call, SMS, email etc) to be queued together

Customer Lifecycle - is a generic term used to describe all interactions points with a customer from acquisition through to default or cancellation

Hang Up – in outbound, a hang up is when a call recipient hangs up immediately (normally within the first 5 seconds of a call)

Home-based agents – is a terms used to describe where the agents work from their home rather than a physical call centre.

Homeshoring (home-shoring) – is a term used to describe 2 different environments. Some companies use it to describe the process of repatriating the call centre to a domestic environment when it has previously been offshored. Other companies use it to describe where calls are handled by home-based call centre agents.

Hot-Key Transfer – is the process of transferring a specific call type to another agent. This is often used in outbound lead generation where the outsourced vendor transfers "hot leads" through to the client's captive centre to finalise certain details. This is often used between offshore outsourced call centres and domestically based captive centres.

In-house call centre – is a term interchangeable with captive call centre.

Lifestyle Surveys - are outbound calls made to generate lists to be used in telesales campaigns. They will ask a customer a series of questions designed to profile them for calls by telesales agents which should then achieve a higher conversion rate than standard cold calling. Most of this is conducted offshore

Multishoring (multi-shoring) – is the term used to describe where call centre operations are deployed in multiple countries.

Multisourcing (multi-sourcing) – is the term used to describe when multiple call centre outsourcing vendors are used across a business.

Nearshoring (near-shoring) – is the term used to describe an offshoring environment where the location the calls are being handled has a close geographical proximity to where the calls are originated. For The UK, this term is often used to describe calls handled in Northern Ireland, The Republic of Ireland or Central & Eastern Europe. For The USA, this term is often used to describe locations such as Mexico, The Dominican Republic or South America.

Net Promoter Score - is a measure used to determine the satisfaction rates among customers

Offshoring – is the term used to describe when a call centre operation is placed in an overseas country. This includes both offshore outsourcing and captive offshore facilities.

Outsourcing – is the term used to describe when a call centre operation is handled by a third party organisation.

Per call billing – is a method by which the call centre outsourcing company charges its clients. The outsourced vendor charges a fee for each call answered regardless of duration. Sometimes, different call types are charged at different rates.

Per minute billing – is the term used to describe where the client of the outsourced vendor is charge a fee for each minute of the call.

PQQ - a PQQ is a pre-qualification questionnaire designed to ascertain basic information from potential outsourcing vendors with a view to them being taken to the next stage of the tender process.

Predictive Dialler - is a telephony technology used in outbound calling which dials a list of telephone numbers, screening out no-replies, engaged tones, answering machines and disconnected numbers while predicting at what point a call centre agents will be able to handle the next call.

Productive hour – is a method of the call centre outsourcing company to bill its clients. A productive hour is where the client is charged a fee per hour for the amount of time the agent is ready and able to make or receive calls.

Quality monitoring - is the process used to ascertain how an agent is performing against a series of pre-defined criteria.

Remote listening - is often referred to as remote monitoring. This is where a client is given the ability to listen to live telephone calls from outside of the call centre

RFI - RFI stands for Request for Information. This is part of the tender process used in the early stages in order to pre-qualify potential outsourcing vendors who are then put through to an RFP

RFP - RFP stands for Request for Proposal. This is the part of the tender where outsourcing vendors who have been pre-qualified are asked to submit a detailed proposal covering aspects such as technology, operational and pricing components.

Rightshoring (right-shoring) – is where a call centre operation is placed in a specific location which is felt will best serve the needs of the operation.

Screen pop - is a feature of a computer telephony integration (CTI) application that automatically displays all of the relevant caller and account information on an agents screen during a call.

Shared agents - agents who make calls for multiple clients

SPH - is short for sales per hour. This is normally calculated as the number of sales made per agent per day

Timesheet hour – is a method of the call centre outsourcing company to bill its clients. It differs from a productive hour in that all of the agents time including things such as training and breaks are charged for. The cost of a timesheet hour is typically 20% lower than a productive hour.

Train the trainer – is often referred to as TTT. This is where the client trains the trainers of the outsourced operation who in turn train the call centre agents and other relevant personnel.

Vendor manager – is a common term used to describe the client representative whose role it is to manage the relationship with the outsourced partner

Voice of the customer - is a term used to define how customers feel about the experience they receive. In the perspective of the call centre, it calculates a number of factors and feeds back on areas of improvement

Workforce Management - are the people (normally within the outsourced vendor) who are responsible for determining headcounts of agents required based on anticipated call flows.

Wrap time - is the time taken at the end of the telephone call to take any post call actions such as entering information into a computerised system

ABOUT THE AUTHOR

Rob O'Malley is a veteran of the outsourced call centre industry having dedicated over 2 decades to improving it. He has worked for major outsourced vendors and established the first UK-centric call centre in Manila back in 2000. He is a regular contributor to publications on both call centre and outsourcing related topics and is the author of the book "Philippines Call Centre Outsourcing". He has been The Chairman of The British Philippine Outsourcing Council since 2008.

www.ingramcontent.com/pod-product-compliance
Lightning Source LLC
Chambersburg PA
CBHW070715180526
45167CB00004B/1489